METH
FAY

D1233917

WRITERS AND THEIR WORKS: NO. 166

ANDREW YOUNG

by LEONARD CLARK

&

R. S. THOMAS

by R. GEORGE THOMAS

Published for The British Council
and the National Book League
by Longmans, Green & Co.

Two shillings and sixpence net

Andrew Young is probably unique among twentieth century poets, for he is a Christian mystic, whose poems on their deepest level are meditations. They are filled with a gentle faith which imbues his love for every bird, beast and plant of the English countryside with a special significance. He writes little and slowly, and formally he is unadventurous; but he is never commonplace. He is a poet of great individuality and quality, and it is the author's belief that Young's *Into Hades* 'is the most powerful long poem in the English language since the publication of T. S. Eliot's *Four Quartets*'.

R. S. Thomas, like Young an Anglican priest, is far removed from the gentler aspects of the English countryside. His life has been spent in a remote hill parish in Wales, and his poems reflect his uncompromising process of self-identification with the inarticulate hill-farmers who had at first filled him with despair. In his later poems, the author shows, the poet's own hard-won understanding of the human lot is an invitation to 'the poetic conscience of a wide English reading public . . . to re-examine the accepted premises of its over-intellectualized way of life'.

Leonard Clark, who writes about Andrew Young, is a poet, editor and broadcaster. He has published an anthology of poems for children, *Drums and Trumpets*, a volume of reminiscences, *Green Wood: A Gloucestershire Childhood*, and a collection of original children's poems, *Daybreak*. He edited *The Collected Poems of Andrew Young*, and a tribute to the poet called *Andrew Young: Prospect of a Poet*.

R. G. Thomas, the author of the essay on R. S. Thomas, is Senior Lecturer in English Language and Literature at University College, Cardiff, and is well-known in Wales as a poet, critic and broadcaster. He is on the editorial board of the *Anglo-Welsh Review*, and has published many articles in Britain, America and the Continent on English writers in Wales.

Bibliographical Series
of Supplements to 'British Book News'
on Writers and Their Work

★

GENERAL EDITOR
Bonamy Dobrée

¶ Thanks are due to Messrs. Rupert Hart-Davis for permission to include quotations from the works of Andrew Young and R. S. Thomas.

ANDREW YOUNG

R. S. THOMAS

ANDREW YOUNG

by
Leonard Clark

★

R. S. THOMAS

by
R. G. Thomas

PUBLISHED FOR
THE BRITISH COUNCIL
AND THE NATIONAL BOOK LEAGUE
BY LONGMANS GREEN & CO.

LONGMANS, GREEN AND CO. LTD.
48 Grosvenor Street, London, W.1

*Associated companies, branches and representatives
throughout the world*

First Published in 1964
© Leonard Clark and
R. G. Thomas 1964

*Printed in Great Britain by
F. Mildner & Sons, London, E.C.1*

ANDREW YOUNG

I

ANDREW Young's reputation as a poet and naturalist has been gained not as a result of strident propaganda by critics but by his own steady, solid, unpretentious performance over the years. It cannot be said of his poetry that it has ever been in, or out of, fashion. And yet, though it has never been boosted, nor cultivated by esoteric cliques, it has always had its admirers, at least since the publication of *Winter Harvest* in 1933. More people, certainly in Britain, have read Andrew Young's books about wild flowers and scenery than his poetry. Perhaps all this is because his poetry defies analysis. One either likes it at a glance, and wants to read more, or, after a first and superficial acquaintance, leaves it to pass on to something else with a different range of subject matter.

But the situation has changed rapidly in recent years. From being one of the dark horses of English poetry, he has now firmly established himself within his own pastoral and religious sphere as one of the finest writers of lyric poetry of this century. His reputation will continue to grow. So long as men continue to honour and read poetry, so long will they turn to poets like Andrew Young for truth and freshness about the countryside, and man's relationship with his God. He has successfully linked the small and humble things of life with the larger and everlasting, so making them part of eternity. He is not merely a naturalist who prefers to express himself in poetic forms: he is a poet, pure, simple.

Andrew Young is in sight of his eightieth birthday, yet, although he has been a writer for over fifty years, his bibliographer will be put to little trouble, for his output in bulk has been small. From the beginning he has been a writer of quality rather than of quantity. His work has always been characterized by expert and often out-of-the-way knowledge, scientifically-accurate observation, and unusual imaginative power. What is more important, perhaps, has been his ability to use the English language simply, precisely, and originally. He is a master of compression, both in speaking and in writing; in his poems he has extracted every shade of sound and meaning from the words he has chosen with such sureness for his purposes. All this adds up to a rare talent.

Young's contribution to literature consists of a dozen or so small books of short nature and religious poems, a verse play, a long eschatological poem, and four books about British wild flowers, scenery, and pastoral poets. In all, he has published just over two hundred poems; it is doubtful if he will write any more.

Andrew Young's earlier poems attracted little attention at the time; nor were they issued by any well-known publishing house. But when he was nearly fifty, the Nonesuch Press published *Winter Harvest*, a collection of forty-five poems, including seventeen which had not previously been published. But although this handful of poems brought wider recognition, his development as a poet has been slow. This is due to a number of factors. To begin with, he is of retiring disposition, he has never pressed his claims (it would not strike him that he had any), he has stood outside all literary 'movements'. And further, though he has been a constant reader of poetry all his life, he has rarely been influenced by much of what he has read. He does not claim much understanding of the work of many of his younger contemporaries. He certainly has no considerable sympathy with the more 'modernistic' elements among them. Finally, he has not often been in the news, but has lived the quiet, unsensational life of a country clergyman for over forty years, and now, in retirement, has settled down in a remote part of the county of Sussex. When all these factors are considered it would have been surprising if so individual a poet had greatly changed his style of writing or extended his range of subject matter. Yet younger contemporaries admit that they have learned much from him in the matter of craftsmanship and control.

Young is a Scot, though he has lived for the greater part of his life in southern England. But his loyalties and traditions remain with the land of his birth, and he has written a great deal about Scotland in prose and poetry. The background of his early years, and his secular and religious education under the Scottish system, should not be forgotten by students of his work. He was born at Elgin on 29 April, 1885, and brought up in a good middle class home. The family moved to Edinburgh two years later and, after a short period at a small private school, Young won a scholarship to the Royal High School there. Here he remained until he was eighteen, took his Leaving Certificate, and then went on to Edinburgh University. He read Latin, Greek, English, Physics, Moral Philosophy, Metaphysics and Fine Art for his Master's degree, and while still a student won a scholarship which took him to Paris to learn more about art, living on the edge of poverty in the Latin quarter. He has never lost his love for art, and he has an informed appreciation of the paintings of the British water colourists.

On leaving the University he was enrolled as a theological student at New College, Edinburgh. His formal education and religious training completed at the late age of twenty-seven, he became a Minister of the United Free Church of Scotland, his first pastorate being at the remote village of Temple in Midlothian. His flock was no more than one hundred and fifty—only slightly less than the size of some of the editions of his first books of poetry. He married in 1914, a son was born a year later, and he himself went to work for six months at a time in France. He was attached to the Y.M.C.A. and lectured to the troops. He had still published only one book of poems. The Great War over, he left Scotland to become Minister of the English Presbyterian Church at Hove, in Sussex, where a daughter was born in 1922. Six small books of poems were published between that year and 1931.

Following the wider recognition of his poetic powers
with the appearance of *Winter Harvest*, Andrew Young's
first *Collected Poems* (no more than a total of 106), and his
verse drama, *Nicodemus*, were published in 1936.

It was about this time that he met Dr. George Bell, Bishop
of Chichester; the result of this meeting was that he joined
the Church of England. After a very brief period of training,
and one curacy, in 1941 he was appointed to the living of
Stonegate, and he remained vicar of this Sussex hamlet until
his retirement eighteen years later. In 1948 he was preferred
to a Canonry of Chichester. He now lives at Yapton, near
Arundel.

While at Stonegate he wrote books about wild flowers
and his travels in search of them: *A Prospect of Flowers* (1945),
A Retrospect of Flowers (1950) and *A Prospect of Britain* (1956);
he published a new edition of his *Collected Poems* (1950), the
long poem *Into Hades* (1952) and, in 1958, *Out of the World
and Back*, which contained *Into Hades* and its sequel, *A
Traveller in Time*. Since he has been living at Yapton he has
published a selection of his poems for children, *Quiet as Moss*
(1959) and the definitive edition of his *Collected Poems* (1960)
consisting of the 209 poems which he wishes to preserve,
with the addition of his play, *Nicodemus*. He has also published one prose work in retirement, *The Poet and the
Landscape* (1962), and is now at work on another which
deals with the poetry of the Bible.

II

Andrew Young's poems, as they appear in the definitive
edition of *Collected Poems*, are largely concerned with the
birds, flowers, trees, rivers, animals, hills, fields, insects,
ruins, and burial places of England and Scotland, as observed
and pondered on by him. The collection is, in short, a
comprehensive record of the places he has visited and the

experiences he has had at those places; it is a geography book as well as a field book of nature study. Neither is the history of these places ignored. Andrew Young has always been powerfully affected by the past, and by the dead. His poems carry many references to burial mounds, druidical circles, old battle grounds, prehistoric peoples, and Roman remains. This acute feeling for archaeology is very marked. As for places, there are, for instance, poems about Romsey Abbey, the Forest of Dean, the Paps of Jura, Teesdale, Sedgemoor, Glencoe, the Fens, the Rivers Tyne, Dove and Erme. They have all been so assimilated that their essential characteristics and atmosphere have become part of the observer who, because he is a poet, has written poems which are much more than skilful flights of charming description. Andrew Young has always related the places he has visited to life itself and recognized what part they have to play in a Christian scheme of things. For instance, in a poem called 'The Stars' there is this:

> If eye can nothing see
> But what is part of me,
> I ask and ask again
> With a persuasive pain,
> What thing, O God, am I
> This mote and mystery?

and in 'The Tumulus':

> No bugle shatters sleep for them, so surely
>   They keep the peace:
> I in their old decease mourn prematurely
>   My own at ease.

The meaning of life, death, and after-death are great and eternal themes proceeding from a consideration of everyday, observable things like stars, a tumulus, a river in spate. But the eyes that have seen them and the mind which broods over them are well-cultivated and disciplined. They *know* much about natural phenomena and are sensitively aware of human behaviour. The heart, too, is full of compassion for what is weak and defenceless.

Poets have always seen correspondences and similarities between like and unlike things. To arrive at truth they sometimes explore opposites and incongruities. None more so than Andrew Young. His poems are full of wit, fancies and conceits, which serve to jerk readers by sudden shock into a realization of some fact or significant thought which, until that moment, has escaped notice and consideration.

Examples of this marked characteristic are observed, for instance, in 'The Dead Bird':

> Ah, that was but the wind
> Your soft down stirred,
> O bird, lying with sidelong head;
> These open eyes are blind,
> I cannot frighten you away;
> You are so very dead
> I almost say
> 'You are not a dead *bird*.'

'These open eyes are blind' and 'You are not a dead *bird*' (making us reflect further on the word 'bird') are typical Andrew Young finger prints.

> But as I think how Death sat once
> And with sly fingers picked those princely bones,
> I feel my bones are verily
> The stark and final I.
> I climb the hill housed in warm flesh,
> But now as one escaped from its false mesh
> Through the wan mist I journey on,
> A clanking skeleton.

The man in this poem, 'The Round Barrow', having considered the royal bones in the barrow, then considers his own, continuing to walk on through life 'a clanking skeleton'. 'The White Blackbird', where the conceit is cunningly contrived and then delivered with enormous power in the last two lines, consists of less than three dozen words:

> Gulls that in meadows stand,
> The sea their native land,
> Are not as white as you
> Flitting from bough to bough
> You who are white as sin
> To your black kith and kin.

One should observe the strength of 'The sea their native *land*' and '*white* as sin'.

It is clear from the poems already noted that the eyes of this poet are trained to a degree of extraordinary exactness. They see down to the last detail but it is the shrewd mind behind them which is able to choose just that which is essential for the reader to take the particular point and message which the poet wishes to communicate. There is, then, the observation, the divining imagination, and then the facility with language. The amalgam makes memorable poetry. There are countless examples of this process. Unseen birds are referred to as 'hidden ventriloquists' in 'The Ventriloquists'; we find 'plump snow' and 'varnished straws' in 'Snow', swallows are called 'blue-winged snow-balls' and 'jugglers with their own bodies' in 'The Swallows'; grubs, 'small priests', in 'The Elm Beetle'; and children, 'small Herods' in 'Children Gathering Violets':

> Children, small Herods, slay these Innocents
> With blue untidy faces and sweet scents.

Andrew Young's ideas, though about common things, are never commonplace. In 'A Wet Day' he writes of how, after a storm of rain in a wood, he hung up his coat and hat on a bough to dry—an ordinary enough experience. Having

done this simple action he felt like 'a snake that had cast off
his slough'. He was free and as elemental as

> the slow black slugs that sprawled abroad
> Making soft shameless love on the open road.

And then he turned round:

> startled I stood
> To see a dead man hanging in the wood;
> By two clear feet of air he swung afloat,
> One who had hanged himself in hat and coat.

And so the poem turns out to be a commentary on the freedom of the spirit, of life after death, a poem of regret that
the writer must continue to live on earth as a man 'in hat
and coat'.

What a curious idea it is, too, in 'Hibernating Snails', to
say that some of the snails sleeping on an ivied tree, 'each
china throat sealed up with glair', will never wake again
because

> From two years old or even three
> They crawled alive to their own funeral.

What force there is in the word 'alive' when associated with
'funeral'.

III

In the matter of versification Young is a traditionalist. He
does not see any good reason why he should abandon rhyme
and metre in order to say what he has to say. Although this
is so, he is capable of considerable variation within the
traditional framework, for his ear, like his eye, is sharp and
true. A close examination of even the briefest of his poems
reveals rhythmic subtleties which make for the greater

understanding and significance of the poem. Most of his poems are short and compact, consisting generally of quatrains, though there are many examples of three, five, and six-lined verses. Many of his most successful poems consist of no more than a single quatrain; few have more than twenty lines. Yet he has neither a limited vocabulary nor an archaic one. He uses English words sparingly but his meaning is always perfectly clear. His verbs are particularly strong as, for instance, in 'The stars *rushed* forth' ('The Stars'), 'roots *roll* through the ground' ('The Oak Wood'), and 'The loud bees *lurched* about the hill' ('The Bee-Orchis'). His adjectives are equally striking: 'I lifted from the ground my grass-pressed hand' ('Palmistry') and 'Look, how the blackthorn now Changes to *trifling* dust upon the bough' ('Stay, Spring'). Add to this fluency and adroitness, a range of imagery, a witty and sometimes sardonic way of looking at things, and it is not difficult to understand why such a poet should not wish to change his style.

What has been said so far, in general, about Andrew Young's short poems is abundantly true when it comes to particularize about a single poem. 'The Flood'—a poem of considerable atmosphere and truth—is a good example:

> The winter flood is out, dully glazing the weald,
> The Adur, a drowned river, lies in its bed concealed;
> Fishes flowing through fences explore paddock and field.
>
> Bushes, waist-deep in water, stand sprinkled here and there;
> A solitary gate, as though hung in mid-air,
> Waits idly open, leading from nowhere to nowhere.
>
> These bushes at night-fall will have strange fish for guests,
> That wagtail, tit and warbler darkened with their nests;
> Where flood strays now, light-headed lapwings lifted crests.
>
> But soon comes spring again; the hazel-boughs will angle
> With bait of yellow catkins that in the loose winds dangle
> And starry scarlet blossoms their blind buds bespangle;

Dogs'-mercury from the earth unfold seed-clasping fists
And green-leaved honeysuckle roll in tumbling twists
And dreams of spring shake all the seeds that sleep in cists.

O blue-eyed one, too well I know you will not awake,
Who waked or lay awake so often for my sake,
Nor would I ask our last leave-taking to retake.

If lesser love of flower or bird waken my song,
It is that greater love, too full to flow along,
Falls like that Adur back, flood-like, silent and strong.

The Adur is a small river in Sussex. In the first verse, the
poet writes of the Adur as 'a drowned river', a strange idea,
which regards the thing that 'drowns', as being itself
'drowned' by flood water. And again, because it is new
territory, the fishes *explore* 'paddock and field'. The picture
of a flooded river is immediately conjured up; the long, easy
flowing lines give a sense of space and distance. It is almost
a Dutch painter's scene, well described both in this and in
the next verse, where the half-submerged bushes stand
'sprinkled here and there', another example of how powerfully the poet uses his verbs. The phrase 'leading from
nowhere to nowhere' suggests confusion and loss, other
themes which are often found in Andrew Young's poems.
In the third verse, we are reminded that where the nests of
wagtail, tit and warbler formerly were, 'strange fish' will
that night take their place, and there is the comparison
between the words 'darkened' (referring to the birds' nests)
and the 'light-headed' lapwings. In the next verse, with the
coming of spring, the hazel-boughs are thought of as fishing
rods because they 'angle with bait of yellow catkins'. The
mood of the poem has quietly changed with the passing of
winter. The river is now almost forgotten, as the poet
remembers with deep grief his dead mother, the 'blue-eyed
one', and the great love which flowed between them, a love
far greater than his for flower or bird, to be compared to the
drowned Adur, so flooded it cannot move. The poet has a
feeling of guilt and insufficiency about all this and does not

wish to remember their last leave-taking. The poem has been worked up very powerfully; it is something much more than a picture, however beautifully painted, of a country river in flood. It is a statement of faith, a poet's philosophy. What the poem has really been leading up to all the time is the belief in, and the recognition of, Love's greater flood, as, in particular, it exists between mother and child.

Andrew Young is a Christian priest and, therefore, believes in the resurrection and the immortality of the human spirit. It is hardly surprising to find that many of his poems are about death, and especially his own death. But for all his superabundant delight in natural phenomena, his concern with death, his paradoxical wit, his love for humanity, he is essentially a poet of deep reverence for his Maker.

IV

His verse mystery play, *Nicodemus*, was first published as a separate book, and was broadcast with incidental music composed by Imogen Holst. It was typical of Young to choose to write a play about the Jewish ruler who came to Jesus by night. The result is a series of dramatic scenes of great beauty and holiness.

The chief characters, after Nicodemus, are John, Peter, Judas, and the priests Caiaphas and Annas. A prelude reveals John, as an old man, writing his Gospel. There follows a scene in which Nicodemus meets John, as a young man, on that windy, full moon night of the visitation to Jesus. He encounters other disciples and a complaining blind man who is also seeking Jesus:

> I will be healed by day;
> I should be only half-healed in the dark.
> My eyes must look up at the blessed sun.
> They say it is no bigger than an apple
> And made of fire. How can a fire be round?

The next scene—after a second short prelude—takes place in the Hall of Hewn Stone. A meeting of the Sanhedrin is about to take place. Before it begins, John beseeches Nicodemus to 'come out into the light as His disciple'. The meeting, which is concerned with the question of what ought to be done about Jesus, is exceedingly stormy. Saul of Tarsus is one of the witnesses. He speaks in Andrew Young riddles. The blind man also appears before the Sanhedrin but no longer blind because Jesus has healed him. And then, vehemently challenged by Annas, Nicodemus is revealed as a follower of Jesus.

A third prelude discovers the aged John still writing his Gospel. The angel who had rolled away the stone in Gethsemane—'the angel of the sepulchre'—now enters and reveals to John that Nicodemus is to be foully slain by the Jews.

The final scene of this tender, moving drama is outside the sepulchre itself where two Temple constables are about to be relieved by two of their fellows. Those on duty talk of having heard music in the air:

> High in the air; sounds without instruments,
> Voices without people, as though the air
> Were playing of itself and singing too.

The former blind man also comes to keep vigil. He is arrested by the constables but not before Nicodemus appears. The solitary watcher now outside the sepulchre, he prays:

> O Jesus, if your spirit haunts this place—
> I feel that you are here, here in this garden,
> Where they have brought and planted your poor body.
> But not to rise again—forgive, forgive me!
> You see me kneeling here, my sin as dark
> As the black shadows of this moon-washed garden.
> I tried and yet I did not try to save you.

The whole of his speech gives one the feeling that it is the priest-poet himself who is speaking. The Temple Guard re-enter with the blind man bound, there is an earthquake, the stone rolls back like a wheel, a lighted altar is disclosed. Christ is risen. The play ends with Nicodemus saying:

> O risen Lord,
> I do not ask you to forgive me now;
> There is no need.
> I came to-night to speak to your dead body,
> To touch it with my hands and say 'Forgive' . . .
> You have forgiven me. It is enough.
> Why do I kneel before your empty tomb?

Nicodemus is Andrew Young's religious testimony in poetry. It is a play about a man's stupidity and fall from grace, a play of hope and forgiveness, of resurrection and immortality, centred on the brave, if hesitant, Nicodemus who believed implicitly but would not come out into the open until it was too late. The three preludes and the three scenes are interspersed with four metrical psalms sung as hymns—a relic of Young's Church of Scotland days.

One poem remains to be commented upon. This is *Out of the World and Back*, published in two parts: the first, *Into Hades*, in 1952, and the second, its sequel, *A Traveller in Time*, in 1958, with a revised *Into Hades* accompanying it.

Into Hades has fourteen sections and begins dramatically. The poet imagines that he has died and on an autumnal day is watching his own funeral in the graveyard of St. Peter's Church in Stonegate, Sussex. Then he

> saw the Three
> Who after the priest's, 'I heard a voice from heaven'
> Drew closer to the grave's brink and gazed down.

His soul (or phantasm) proceeds on its journey:

> I stared in wonder
> At what had the appearance of a prison . . .
> Reaching out my hand
> To put it to the proof, I touched a stone;
> It was as soft as mist; my hand went through it.

The prison is symbolic of the womb. Assuming, as it were, another body he hovers backwards and forwards between his youth and his later years. He begins to haunt the church of which he had been incumbent. A celebration of the Holy Communion is about to begin:

> As the candle flames, indignant eyes, burn through it,
> I slid down from the tree; not church, but churchyard,
> Fitted a ghost. I was excommunicated.

He has been 'locked out by St. Peter's key'. He is present at Mattins when

> The fog had left the sun
> A heavy dew to lift; Thomson, the farmer,
> Trailed a dark track in the cow-pasture.

This remarkable poem for all its deep learning, its reference to remote scholars and mystics, is full of such homely touches. It has, too, many of Andrew Young's characteristic twists of thought:

> Which should we be in heaven,
> Our parents' children or our children parents?
> We might be both.

But, above all, it is a poem of a bracing, beginning-of-the-world, dawn chilliness. The strange adventure continues. The poet inherits a new and mystical body and has visions of a new earth and heaven. Of this new earth Young writes:

> Her beauty sparkled;
> Though I knew her for the old earth, now renewed,
> Reborn, she was so transfigured, so unearthly,
> I felt I tarnished her even with looking.

And of the new heaven:

> I clutched at symbols;
> The sky a mirror, feet moving to and fro.
> An albatross, a fountain rising in prayer,
> One who bent over me, tall as a pillar,
> Reflected faces, swaying like flowers.

So back to the grave, and the old earth, and the exploration ends.

Into Hades is the most powerful long poem in the English language since the publication of T. S. Eliot's *Four Quartets*. Its strange beauty, its sense of the unexpected and high lyrical quality do not cut it off, however, from Young's shorter poems. The unusual theme and the range of symbols are handled with sureness of touch and with perfect control of phrase and cadence. It is a poem almost devoid of mannerisms.

A Traveller in Time has thirteen sections. It begins with the poet of *Into Hades* back once more in the world, though still in ghost-like form. He sets out now on a new voyage of spiritual discovery going back into time, searching out the roots of religion. He first finds himself in a wooded dell when a man suddenly crosses his path:

> But was he a man and walking?
> All I saw was a head and shoulders!
> Herod was not so startled
> By the Baptist's head on a charger.

This half-man accompanies him as he becomes the traveller in time. Then he is present at a passage of arms in a medieval tiltyard where the religion of love is being enacted. After the tournament, he finds himself in an abbey, witnessing the religion of sacrifice and worship, of martyrs and saints. The abbey vanishes, and we are now by a nymph's well in ancient Greece. There is a procession with 'a God in the farmwagon drawn by white oxen', and then the Eleusinian Mysteries and the ancient orgies associated with them. There follows rebirth from the robes of Demeter and then, in that dread Hall at Eleusis:

> Retreating to a corner,
> I stood by one, an old initiate,
> Who viewed the scene with disillusioned eyes.
> I felt he would have said, if he had spoken:
> *All is the effort to accomplish death,*
> *The returning to the safety of the womb,*
> *First and last love.*

This, then, is what this poem is mostly about. 'First and last love' lie in 'the safety of the womb' which is the real and true love.

The traveller in time, in motion once again, with the half-man never very far from him, arrives in the Palestine of Hosea's days and to the witnessing of Hosea's buying back of Gomer, his wife, who was a sacred prostitute in the House of Baal. This then is the love of acceptance.

So from the land of rocks to the town of Nazareth where the half-man is dramatically revealed, at an electrifying point of the poem, as the brother who had died before the poet could ever know him—the one who had gone on before into journeying in time and, therefore, knew something of what the poet was experiencing:

> Shadowy shapes
> Looming through pallid air, nothing distinct,
> Was all I saw, when he caught me in his arms,
> Startled, half-frightened. 'I am that dead brother
> You never knew', he said, and added quickly,
> Thrusting me off, 'We are in Nazareth;
> Watch for a woman; she carries Christ in her womb'.

The Christ is born, the Light itself made manifest, and prophecy is revealed in Mary.

The journey draws to a close with the Temptations in the desert. The poem becomes even richer with imaginative detail. There is the Transfiguration, Jerusalem on the day of Calvary, and then the realization that the phantasm is at last to be disintegrated. There is a moving description of the Crucifixion—the climax of the poem—when the traveller, having explored and savoured the many expressions and forms of love through the ages realizes, with burning conviction, that, at Calvary

> All other loves,
> That in my trivial travels I had witnessed
> Were thin outcroppings of the primal love
> The creative Word imparted to the world.

And last of all, the twentieth century traveller in time is back in the dale of the second section of the poem to meet Richard Rolle, the mystic, who is writing *The Fire of Love*. The poem, conceived as an act of worship to God, now rises to a tremendous mystical climax. The poet soars to the stars and beyond them in an exultant note of supreme ecstasy with hope and longings:

> Soon I should learn;
> The ghost must go; the cocoon spun by the worm,
> The butterfly would burst. New eyes would see
> The invisible world into which my brother vanished.

Young, for all his concern with the creatures of this world, is revealed as the poet of 'the invisible world'.

V

Andrew Young has published four books of prose, *A Prospect of Flowers* (1945), *A Retrospect of Flowers* (1950), *A Prospect of Britain* (1956), and *The Poet and the Landscape*

(1962). Each book has taken him five years to write and each is complementary to his poetry. They are records of his travels in Great Britain in search of wild flowers, and signify his familiarity with the more unusual places of these islands. These books show him to be a creature of mountains and moors, of the lesser-known counties, a wanderer in mist and chill, birds and small animals his only company. But the books are more than these. They are little works of erudition, of extraordinary fascinating detail, revealing a remarkable knowledge of literature, history, botany and folklore. And yet they are never boring, because of the warm humanity of the writing and the shy personality which is always peeping through. Andrew Young has the unusual gift of being able to communicate his interests and enthusiasms to the ordinary reader. He writes of flowers and the countryside with such love and power that he can hold the interest of those who know little, or care little, about these things.

A Prospect of Flowers begins with a chapter called, 'How it began'. We are told that it was the result of Andrew Young playing truant while at school, when he discovered a wild flower at Cramond, a hamlet on the Firth of Forth. It was a speedwell. 'Speedwell, name of happy omen! It sped me on a long journey from the sand-dunes of Norfolk to the cliffs of Cornwall, from the bogs of the New Forest to the mountains of Angus.' And that journey, so happily shared with his readers, introduces them to winter heliotrope, snowdrops, dog's mercury, daisies, lilies, wild orchids, trees and shrubs—some common, many rare. All these are portrayed against a background of the seasons, interspersed with anecdotes and profuse quotation. In fact, the book is an anthology, a storehouse of strange knowledge, with essays on botanists and botanophiles, the names of spring flowers, the morals of plants and the botany of poets. In some ways the book is his best biography, a book of acute perception, of patient, modest searching, of truth sought, and truth found.

A Retrospect of Flowers covers the same kind of ground. More is revealed of the poet and of his travels in search of plants and of his respect for the botanist, for he has never claimed that he himself is one. In this book we are introduced to dandelions, gorse, primrose, bluebells, violets, to flowers in spring, to the art of collecting plants so as not to hurt their feelings, to small and tall trees, flowers in Scotland and in all parts of England. There is a whole chapter devoted to the small butterfly orchid and another to the flowers of the hayfield and of the kitchen garden. *A Retrospect of Flowers* is as full of quotations and allusions as the first book and shows the same intimate and loving knowledge of people, plants and places.

A Prospect of Britain, though in similiar strain, is more comprehensive. It is an enthralling record of numerous visits paid by Andrew Young in search of plants all over the country. Here are the personal and accurate observations of an informed traveller who has seen much and missed little, who has visited the corners and crannies of the countryside and who is able to describe his experiences with no preconceived ideas. Beginning with a chapter on English inns, he ranges from the Cotswolds to Edinburgh, from Haworth and the Yorkshire dales to the Lizard, from Hardy's Wessex to Kirkcudbright, from St. David's to the Isles of Scilly. This prospect of Britain is a prospect of the little-known and the unfamiliar. There are few cities or large conurbations mentioned, but many cathedrals, villages, forests, lakes and characters. As ever, the writing is friendly, informal, witty and humorous. It is, perhaps, the most readable of all Young's prose works, the way, perhaps, all guides to a territory ought to be written.

Young's most recent prose book is *The Poet and the Landscape*. This consists of a series of brilliant chapters about English pastoral poets as seen in their authentic rural settings. The book, overflowing with information and frank opinions about the poets and the places where they live, is an exciting anthology of quite unusual beauty and charm.

The poets include John Clare, Hogg, Hardy, Wordsworth, Cotton and Tennyson. The book is filled with the smell, too, of summer pastures, little lanes and bare uplands.

These books are the work of a superb poet with the keenest of eyes and the liveliest of pens, the life offering of a ceaseless pilgrim, a silent though discerning discoverer. Few poets of our own day have compressed so much into so little. But for all his economy of language and pawky humour, Andrew Young is a poet of great feeling and vision. He has not only described the British countryside with accurate and loving eye and ear but also interpreted it in terms of an unflinching Christian faith. He has seen similarities where apparently none exist and fastened on insignificant details and made them significant. He cannot be dismissed as a mere nature poet in the English pastoral tradition: there is too much of the metaphysical in him for that, too much of the constant questioner. He is unwilling to accept outward appearances alone. He sees beyond the simple elements of this world; and through a few cracks into Eternity, peers for a while into what is Infinite and unknown.

ANDREW YOUNG
A Select Bibliography
(Place of publication London, unless stated otherwise)

Collected Works:

COLLECTED POEMS (1936).

COLLECTED POEMS (1950).

COLLECTED POEMS (1960)

—with a bibliographical note by L. Clark and wood-engravings by J. Hassall. Awarded the Duff Cooper Memorial Prize.

Selected Works:

WINTER HARVEST (1933). *Verse*

QUIET AS MOSS (1959). *Verse*

—chosen by L. Clark, with wood-engravings by J. Hassall.

Separate Works:

SONGS OF NIGHT (1910). *Verse*

BOAZ AND RUTH (1920). *Verse*

THE DEATH OF ELI (1921). *Verse*

THIRTY-ONE POEMS (1922). *Verse*

THE ADVERSARY (1923). *Drama*

—plays in verse.

THE BIRD-CAGE (1926). *Verse*

THE CUCKOO-CLOCK (1929). *Verse*

THE NEW SHEPHERD (1931). *Verse*

THE WHITE BLACKBIRD (1935). *Verse*

NICODEMUS (1937). *Drama*

—a Mystery play in verse.

SPEAK TO THE EARTH (1939). *Verse*

A PROSPECT OF FLOWERS (1945). *Topography*

THE GREEN MAN (1947). *Verse*

A RETROSPECT OF FLOWERS (1950). *Topography*

INTO HADES (1952). *Verse*

A PROSPECT OF BRITAIN (1956). *Topography*

—with photographs by J. Allan Cash.

OUT OF THE WORLD AND BACK (1958). *Verse*

—contains a new poem, 'A Traveller in Time' and 'Into Hades' (previously published 1952).

THE POET AND THE LANDSCAPE (1962). *Topography*

—a series of portraits of English pastoral poets as seen in their own rural settings.

Critical Study:

ANDREW YOUNG: PROSPECT OF A POET (1957), edited by L. Clark —tributes by fourteen writers.

R. S. THOMAS

R. S. Thomas was born in Cardiff in 1913 and was reared and educated in Holyhead, Anglesey. In the mid-thirties he studied Classics at the University College, Bangor and then, after a period of theological training at St. Michael's College, Llandaff, and a few years as a curate, he became Vicar of Manafon in Merionethshire early in the Second World War. His parishioners were principally hill farmers, Welsh-speaking and Nonconformist; their life was a hard struggle for existence against poor terrain, isolation, gradual depopulation and an inhospitable climate. The young priest had studied the native literary language as a first, necessary step towards fulfilling his cure of souls, and, at this time, he seems to have been attracted towards the rapidly developing Welsh nationalist movement. He had been impressed by the literary achievement of some Scottish writers who were grouped around Hugh MacDiarmid, and in 1946 he made some interesting comments which throw light on these formative influences.[1]

One announcement of his initial volume of poems, *The Stones of the Field* (1946), proclaimed it as 'a collection of verse which seeks to re-affirm man's affinity with the age-old realities of stone, field, and trees. These are essentially nature poems, but they are not written in the English tradition. Their imagery is more akin to that of those early Welsh writers, whose clarity of vision was born out of an almost mystical attachment to their environment.' In the same year R. S. Thomas published the following paragraph in an article on 'Some Contemporary Scottish Writing':

There can be no national art without a people, and there can be no people without artists to create them and give form to their dreams and aspirations. This seems to me the crux of the matter. The poet's chief problem is, how in virtue of his mind and vision can he best save his country—directly through political action, or indirectly through his

[1] *Wales*, vol. VI, No. 3 (1946).

creative work? Failure to resolve this difficulty leads to frustration and inertia . . . We have to face the possibility not, I think, of the disappearance of Welsh, but of its inadequacy as a medium for expressing the complex phantasmagoria of modern life. But if we choose English as that medium, have we the singleness of mind, the strength of will to remain primarily Welshmen? Ireland has done it, Scotland is striving after it, and we should do the same.

At this time the poet lived in constant realization of the fact that 'he lives in or belongs to a country of great age, that by geography and tradition has developed an individual way of life'. And he asks himself the rhetorical question: 'After all, why chant the praise of Helen, when Nest remains unsung? Why lament Troy fallen, when Mathrafal lies in ruins?' The classical scholar, it would seem, had fallen under the spell of a new literature—that of medieval Wales—and was in love with his enchanter.

II

As so frequently happens, the poet's prose statements about his poetic intention run somewhat contrary to the reader's actual experience of his verse. R. S. Thomas's two privately published volumes of verse (*The Stones of the Field* and *An Acre of Land*) contain a number of poems on directly Welsh national themes, but many of these have been omitted from his first volume of collected verse, *Song at the Year's Turning* (1955), which is devoted to his poems composed between 1942 and 1954. Neither are there many such distinctly Welsh poems in *Poetry for Supper* (1958), although quite a few appear in *Tares* (1962). The simple truth is that, although R. S. Thomas rarely writes about non-native subjects, he has eschewed specifically political themes and has not been very successful in writing either about Nest or Mathrafal. He found the distinctive subject for his verse in the life of the hill farmers of his parish in the Welsh wilderness. At first he disliked and abused them, but, as his verse developed in power and intensity, a process of self-identification began to develop between the poet and the peasant-farmer, until it could be said, with as much certainty as is possible in critical interpretation, that one of these peasants (Iago Prytherch) became the medium through whose eyes and mouth the poet learned to interpret the world around and within him.

On his first poetic appearance Iago is almost a war-time poster, a mere gloss from the past; he is both a creative footnote to destruction and annihilation and an opportunity for the poet-teacher to try out his gift of invective:

> Yet this is your prototype, who, season by season,
> Against siege of rain and the wind's attrition,
> Preserves his stock, an impregnable fortress
> Not to be stormed even in death's confusion.
> Remember him then, for he, too, is a winner of wars,
> Enduring like a tree under the curious stars.

There are many peasants like Iago scattered throughout Thomas's verse. They guarantee the continuation of an older, and more highly regarded, way of life. They supply the poet with the proof, which he desperately needs, to support his belief that some vision which transcends politics is necessary to the Welsh poet:

For it is England, the home of the industrial revolution, and the consequent twentieth-century rationalism, that have been the winter on our native pastures, and we must break their grip, and the grip of all the quislings and yes-men before we can strike the authentic note . . . Before the awful levelling process of modern uniformity and centralization, the cultivation of one's own poetic individuality, however integrating to the personality, however charming to a few admirers, is a sign of the failure to grow up and begin the wooing of a more exacting lover.[1]

With a remarkable integrity of purpose and a controlled clarity of vision, R. S. Thomas learned to keep political

[1] *Wales*, vol. VI, No. 3 (1946).

attitudes out of his poetry, despite these impassioned prose declarations. The poet pleads for no line of political action and advocates no party platform; instead he seeks to submit to scrutiny the archetypal and basic qualities of rural Welshmen who, by their very isolation and the nature of their occupation, should represent, in almost laboratory conditions, the native vices and virtues:

> I am the farmer, stripped of love
> And thought and grace by the land's harshness.

> You cannot live in the present,
> At least not in Wales.
> There is the language for instance,
> The soft consonants
> Strange to the ear.

Of course *Song at the Year's Turning* contains poems of a different kind, which are based on the glorious and ancient past of Wales as seen in legend and literature; but this is a secondary theme. The principal subject of the volume is the harshness of rural Wales, as presented with compelling eloquence by a priest who castigates and disapproves of his people. A long radio ode ('The Minister') helps to round out the poet's portrait of contemporary Wales. It tells the life-story of a Welsh Nonconformist minister in this wild, lonely countryside of Merioneth. In this ode, Thomas, an Anglican priest, attempts an assessment of the beliefs and attitudes of the dissenters who form the majority of practising Christians in Wales. The resulting picture is acid, partial and satirical; few nonconformists of industrial South Wales would recognize this portrait of themselves. But this caricature—for so I believe it to be—completed Thomas's honest attempt to find poetic terms in which to depict his countrymen. Though the writing is slack and quite untypical of the rest of *Song at the Year's Turning*, it represents a *terminus ad quem* in Thomas's poetic development.

III

The watershed in R. S. Thomas's verse has not been sufficiently recognized. The poems composed before 1952 are, in a very real sense, chronicles of a parish or scenes from rural Merioneth life. Only very occasionally in these poems the poet descends from his pulpit and uncovers, momentarily, the operation of Christian charity which lies beneath the pitiless unmasking of the peasants:

> You will forgive, then, my initial hatred,
> My first intolerance of your uncouth ways,
> You who are indifferent to all that I can offer
> Caring not whether I blame or praise.
>
> The dirt is under my cracked nails:
> The tale of my life is smirched with dung;
> The phlegm rattles. But what I am saying
> Over the grasses rough with dew
> Is, Listen, listen, I am a man like you.

All these poems from the poet's first decade—in *The Stones of the Field* and *An Acre of Land*—derive their strength and power from the cross-tension that exists between the peasant, tied to his soil, and the priest, tied to his people. These poems introduced a strange and novel note into English war poetry, or, indeed, into any mid twentieth-century English poetry that expressed social themes. So much of the social and political verse of the nineteen-thirties was apparently about industrial employment—or the lack of it—but the millennial utterances of many of those poets were so many febrile gestures inspired by a sense of doom and all-devouring Time. The themes of R. S. Thomas belong to a different world. By the very nature of their separate offices, the farmer and the priest are freed from the incessant pressure of temporal haste. This genuine freedom from rush is a significant quality of Thomas's earlier poetry.

All his best poems are clear, momentary statements which are set against a background of timelessness: each scene, and each character in that scene, is caught and held as if by a painter, once and for all time:

> Consider this man in the field beneath,
> Gaitered with mud, lost in his own breath,
> Without joy, without sorrow,
> Without children, without wife,
> Stumbling insensitively from furrow to furrow,
> A vague somnambulist; but hold your tears,
> For his name also is written in the Book of Life.
>
> A man is in the fields, let us look with his eyes
> As the first clouds ripen with the sunrise,
> At the earth around us, marking the nameless flowers
> That minister to him through the tedious hours
> Of sweat and toil, their grave, half-human faces
> Lifted in vain to greet him where he passes.

In each of these quotations, and in many more poems, there is a close resemblance to a Wordsworthian habit: the sudden 'freezing' of a scene which had coincided with the initial moment of poetic inspiration that had given rise to the poem. The poet is continually addressing the reader, placing him in the correct spot for observation, presenting him with the true angle of perspective, and inviting the reader's comment or assent. In a phrase, these earlier poems of R. S. Thomas are a three-cornered wrestle in words between the expressed object of the poet's initial act of perception, the selective and mutative process of the poet's consciousness, and the induced reaction of the reader. Is, then, 'contemplation' too strong a word to describe the action which R. S. Thomas expects, or exacts, from his readers? The answer to this question must wait upon a closer examination of the structure of his poems.

In a sense the exercise of reading through the entire body of his verse can be likened to the slow progress of an art student through a picture gallery devoted to the works of

one artist. Now, the poet who relies to an excessive degree
on the habit of conveying *in words* the seen world of his own
private angle of vision must necessarily set stringent terms
for the ready (or contemplative) acceptance and appreciation
of his poetry. With some justice Coleridge called sight the
'most despotic' of the senses. If a poet concentrates excessively
on visual effects—be it a pair of ragged claws, a falcon
swooping in its pride, or the precise confusion of Belinda's
dressing table—he may, for a moment, sharpen the focus of
the reader's attention; he also runs the risk of limiting that
free-play of the reader's subconscious attention to the verse
which is a primary condition not only of contemplative
activity but also for the more usual reader-participation in
the poet's verse.

Many of R. S. Thomas's poems which were composed
before 1952 suffer, in part, from the visual limitation which
they imposed upon the reader's attention; yet even in them
Thomas was not leading the reader towards a contemplative
act. Rather the poet was learning to extend the scope of his
poetry to include a genuine experience of communication
between himself and the reader by engaging the reader
openly in some sort of conversation about the subject of his
poetry. Too frequently, at this early stage, the poet adopts
the hortatory manner of the pulpit:

> Remember him, then, for he, too, is a winner of wars.

> You are betrayed by wilderness within,
> That spreads upward and outward like a stain.

>   Is this the way
> You welcome your man from his long mowing
> Of the harsh, unmannerly, mountain hay?

These direct appeals to the reader help to soften both the
starkness of the subject and the sharply etched manner of the
poet: they cushion the shock of the impact of the severe
object upon which we have been asked to gaze. In fact a

constant demand for the reader's support and affirmation pervades the whole gallery of Thomas's portraits and this demand makes possible a shared communion of interest. The immediate success of *Song at the Year's Turning* is the clearest proof that R. S. Thomas's poetry had 'come through'. The private and local world of the poetry, which has evolved in this peculiarly factual way from the need to fulfil a clearly expressed political purpose, has been made available to the wider audience of English readers with no knowledge of Nest and no interest in commemorating the fall of Mathrafal.

IV

To view the poetic development of *Poems 1942–1952* in this way is not a fanciful trope. R. S. Thomas regards himself as the elected voice of this race of men whose way of life has a value which is misunderstood because they lack the art of communication. 'Your silence most offends me', says Don Pedro to Beatrice in *Much Ado About Nothing;* R. S. Thomas makes the same point repeatedly about his peasants, who are ignorant of the ancient ritual behind their daily toil:

> And then at night see him fixed in his chair
> Motionless, except when he leans to gob in the fire.
> There is something frightening in the vacancy of his mind.
>
> No speech; the raised hand affirms
> All that is left unsaid
> By the mute tongue and the unmoistened lips.
>
> Blind? Yes, and deaf, and dumb, and the last irks most,
> For could he speak, would not the glib tongue boast
> A lore denied our neoteric sense,
> Being handed down from the age of innocence?

pulpiteering manner yields in his later verse to a more conversational tone which has broadened the scope of his subjects and which has enabled him to handle Welsh themes without obvious poeticisms—the weakness of the early nationalistic poems; and, what is more, this extension of interest takes place without any diminution of the sharpness of his vision or any slackening of the taut rhythmic structure of his verse. Furthermore, the poet is now able to write about his function as a priest with no sense of divided loyalty, no awkwardness, and no obtrusion of an alien tone into the verse.

A growing assurance in handling colloquial speech rhythms is clearly visible in the post-1952 verse. In the title poem, 'Poetry for Supper', the form of the poem is a dialogue between two old poets who are discussing the nature of poetry: one says:

> Man, you must sweat
> And rhyme your guts taut, if you'd build
> Your verse a ladder.

Immediately, the other replies:

> You speak as though
> No sunlight ever surprised the mind
> Groping on its cloudy path.

Again, 'Expatriates' is conceived as a non-dramatic monologue in reply to a question; it begins:

> Not British: certainly
> Not English. Welsh
> With all the associations
> Black hair and black heart
> Under a smooth skin,
> Sallow as vellum; sharp
> Of bone and wit that is turned
> As a knife against us.

'Anniversary' is a personal, spoken tribute to nineteen years of marriage:

> Nineteen years now
> Under the same roof
> Eating our bread
> Using the same air . . .
>
> Opening the womb
> Softly to let enter
> The one child
> With his huge hunger.

'A Welsh Testament' is a defensive statement and not a political creed in verse:

> All right, I was Welsh. Does it matter?
> I spoke the tongue that was passed on
> To me in the place I happened to be.

The argument is implicit in the poem's structure. We are listening to voices in a debate, until gradually the 'I' of the poem makes his own statement quite naturally in the context of the discussion. Similarly, all the later poems about Iago Prytherch are dialogues between the mature poet and his *alter ego*: 'Could I have said he was the scholar of the fields' pages' or merely 'nature's fool?' For R. S. Thomas now recognizes the potential danger inherent in this habit of turning inward upon himself in search of Prytherch. Is he afraid of becoming merely and solely the laureate of this one, limited man whom he has created?

> Prytherch, I am undone;
> The past calls with the cool smell
> Of autumn leaves, but the mind draws
> Me onward blind with the world's dust
> Seeking a spring that my heart fumbles.

The pun on 'spring' runs sharply counter to the nostalgic picture of autumn and 'the good old days'; despite the poem's explicit rejection of earlier attitudes, in the poet's conscious mind Prytherch continues to stand for a definite, astringent attitude towards the writing of verse. Ultimately, in 'Absolution', the poet merges his own identity with the sinner seeking absolution from a priest, and, by some mysterious metamorphosis, Prytherch, the *alter ego*, has changed places with the poet, who in real life is a priest. For in this poem the priest *is* Prytherch, at his

> stone altar on which the light's
> Bread is broken at dusk and dawn;

it is the poet who asks forgiveness for the 'thin scorn' of his earlier verse. He has worn his soul bare 'on the world's roads' and he has now returned like a prodigal to find Prytherch 'in the same field in which you started'. The poem ends with the peace of returning expressed in religious terms:

> And now come with the first stars
> Big on my lids westward to find
> With the slow lifting up of your hand
> No welcome, only forgiveness.

In these fine lines, with their compressed, emotional intensity, we are once more back in the timeless world of the earlier poems, except that, instead of picture-gazing and exhortation, there is now speech and communion.

V

For the last twenty years R. S. Thomas has added a new colour to the broad spectrum of contemporary English verse and, since 1952, his verse has reached a wide audience through its regular appearance in periodicals. Its formal qualities are unmistakable and are remarkably consistent. A strong visual sense is conveyed to the reader in hard taut rhythms which are dominated by monosyllables and riveted together by short, alliterative phrases, e.g., *day's dirt, tall tree, huge hunger, dead day, race root*. Each subject is presented with a fierce honesty of inward vision—a truly innocent eye—which refuses to blink at the crudities and violence of rural and natural life. Prytherch may dissociate himself from the invaders on his farm with these words:

> I cannot dawdle
> Along their banks and fish in their quick stream
> With crude fingers;

his creator is not so finicky; for him

> A sense of smell is of less importance
>
> Than a sense of balance, walking on clouds
> Through holes in which you can see the earth
>
> Like a rich man through the eye of a needle.
> The mind has its own level to find.

Herein lies the secret of R. S. Thomas's best poetry. The mind is always in control of the verse, yet, underneath the control, are warring emotions: fierce hatred, deep compassion, and a priest's daily exercise in rigorous self-examinations. But the poet's hard-won understanding of the human lot is clarified and interpreted for the modern reader in terms of the husbandman's age-old love-hate relationship with the soil—the source of toil, sorrow, desire, and spiritual anguish. The conversation between the poet and the creatures of his imaginative world is offered clearly and starkly to the reader for his own consideration, reflection, and participation. The poet's initial, myopic concern with his own parishioners is gradually extended to include a wider community. The experience which began as an exercise in observation and contemplation and which developed into a ruthless act of national dissection, gradually became a variation on the theme of the ivory tower of the poet in a twentieth century community and, finally, a series of conversations about deadly sins and the need for forgiveness.

The poet's path towards vital issues has been circuitous but progressive. He began, one must conclude, in conscious imitation of Scottish and Irish writers who were in stated opposition to 'the English urban and mechanized civilization'. His rhetorical cry: 'Why lament Troy fallen, when Mathrafal lies in ruin?' suggests the emergence of a national poet, writing on national themes for a nation that needed a stern awakening. His achievement to date is something quite different: the chronicler of a distant Welsh parish now points his sharp finger at the poetic conscience of a wide English reading public and invites it to re-examine the accepted premisses of its over-intellectualized way of life. Yet the poet's call to contemplate and examine a dying way of life is not an act of nostalgia: this poetry abounds in thinly-disguised comments on our urban and industrial civilization:

> What to do? Stay green.
> Never mind the machine,
> Whose fuel is human souls.
> Live large, man, and dream small.

The chronicler of a parish has become a significant mid-century English poet.

R. S. THOMAS
A Select Bibliography

(Place of publication London, unless stated otherwise)

Selected Works:

THE STONES OF THE FIELD. Carmarthen (1946).

AN ACRE OF LAND. Newtown (1952).

SONG AT THE YEAR'S TURNING: POEMS 1942–1954 (1955)
—with an introduction by J. Betjeman.

POETRY FOR SUPPER: NEW POEMS (1958).

TARES: POEMS (1961).

THE PENGUIN MODERN POETS I: LAWRENCE DURRELL, ELIZABETH JENNINGS, R. S. THOMAS (1962).

THE BREAD OF TRUTH (1963).

Note: The magazine *Wales*, edited by K. Rhys, 2nd series, 1943-5, and Vols. V-VIII, 1954-8, contains many poems and articles by R. S. Thomas, and there are many early poems in *Life and Letters*, Vols. 36-58, 1943-48.

Some Critical and Biographical Studies:

'The New Anglo-Welsh', by G. Jones, *The Welsh Anvil*, 1 (1949).

'The Poetry of R. S. Thomas', by C. Price, *The Welsh Anvil*, 4 (1952).

'Since 1950: R. S. Thomas', by W. M. Merchant, *The Critical Quarterly*, II, No. 4 (1960).

'The Poetry of R. S. Thomas', by R. G. Thomas, *A Review of English Literature*, III, No. 4 (1962).

WRITERS AND THEIR WORK

General Editor: BONAMY DOBRÉE

The first 55 issues in the Series appeared under the General Editorship of T. O. BEACHCROFT

THOMAS HARDY: R. A. Scott-James
HAZLITT: J. B. Priestley
HOOD: Laurence Brander
G. M. HOPKINS: Geoffrey Grigson
T. H. HUXLEY: William Irvine
KEATS: Edmund Blunden
LAMB: Edmund Blunden
LANDOR: G. Rostrevor Hamilton
MACAULAY: G. R. Potter
MEREDITH: Phyllis Bartlett
JOHN STUART MILL: M. Cranston
WILLIAM MORRIS: P. Henderson
NEWMAN: J. M. Cameron
PATER: Iain Fletcher
PEACOCK: J. I. M. Stewart
ROSSETTI: Oswald Doughty
RUSKIN: Peter Quennell
SIR WALTER SCOTT: Ian Jack
SHELLEY: Stephen Spender
R. L. STEVENSON: G. B. Stern
SWINBURNE: H. J. C. Grierson
TENNYSON: F. L. Lucas
THACKERAY: Laurence Brander
FRANCIS THOMPSON: P. Butter
TROLLOPE: Hugh Sykes Davies
OSCAR WILDE: James Laver
WORDSWORTH: Helen Darbishire

Twentieth Century:

W. H. AUDEN: Richard Hoggart
HILAIRE BELLOC: Renée Haynes
ARNOLD BENNETT: F. Swinnerton
EDMUND BLUNDEN: Alec M. Hardie
ELIZABETH BOWEN: Jocelyn Brooke
ROBERT BRIDGES: J. Sparrow
ROY CAMPBELL: David Wright
JOYCE CARY: Walter Allen
G. K. CHESTERTON: C. Hollis
WINSTON CHURCHILL: John Connell
R.G.COLLINGWOOD: E. W. F. Tomlin
I. COMPTON-BURNETT:
          Pamela Hansford Johnson
JOSEPH CONRAD: Oliver Warner
WALTER DE LA MARE: K. Hopkins
THE DETECTIVE STORY IN
          BRITAIN: Julian Symons
NORMAN DOUGLAS: Ian Greenlees

T. S. ELIOT: M. C. Bradbrook
FIRBANK & BETJEMAN: J. Brooke
FORD MADOX FORD: Kenneth Young
E. M. FORSTER: Rex Warner
CHRISTOPHER FRY: Derek Stanford
JOHN GALSWORTHY: R. H. Mottram
ROBERT GRAVES: M. Seymour Smith
GRAHAM GREENE: Francis Wyndham
L. P. HARTLEY & ANTHONY POWELL:
          P. Bloomfield and B. Bergonzi
A. E. HOUSMAN: Ian Scott-Kilvert
ALDOUS HUXLEY: Jocelyn Brooke
HENRY JAMES: Michael Swan
JAMES JOYCE: J. I. M. Stewart
RUDYARD KIPLING: B. Dobrée
D. H. LAWRENCE: Kenneth Young
C. DAY LEWIS: Clifford Dyment
WYNDHAM LEWIS: E. W. F. Tomlin
KATHERINE MANSFIELD: Ian Gordon
JOHN MASEFIELD: L. A. G. Strong
SOMERSET MAUGHAM: J. Brophy
EDWIN MUIR: J. C. Hall
J. MIDDLETON MURRY: Philip Mairet
GEORGE ORWELL: Tom Hopkinson
POETS OF 1939-45 WAR:
          R. N. Currey
POWYS BROTHERS: R. C. Churchill
J. B. PRIESTLEY: Ivor Brown
HERBERT READ: Francis Berry
BERTRAND RUSSELL: Alan Dorward
BERNARD SHAW: A. C. Ward
EDITH SITWELL: John Lehmann
OSBERT SITWELL: Roger Fulford
C. P. SNOW: William Cooper
STRACHEY: R. A. Scott-James
SYNGE & LADY GREGORY:
          E. Coxhead
EDWARD THOMAS: Vernon Scannell
DYLAN THOMAS: G. S. Fraser
G. M. TREVELYAN: J. H. Plumb
WAR POETS: 1914-18:
          Edmund Blunden
EVELYN WAUGH: Christopher Hollis
H. G. WELLS: Montgomery Belgion
CHARLES WILLIAMS:
          John Heath-Stubbs
VIRGINIA WOOLF: Bernard Blackstone
W. B. YEATS: G. S. Fraser